ISBN-13:978-1976175473

To Kharvelle, you have come such a long way. I am so fortunate to be on this journey with you. Be mindful little one. I love you so much.

Rise and shine little puppy!
Run! Run! Run!

Be mindful of where you're running!
Or you'll run into a pond!

Swim around little fish!
Swish! Swish! Swish!

Be mindful of where you're swimming
or you'll swim into a flower pot!

Butterfly butterfly
Float! float! float!

Be mindful of where you're flying
or you'll fly into a potato!

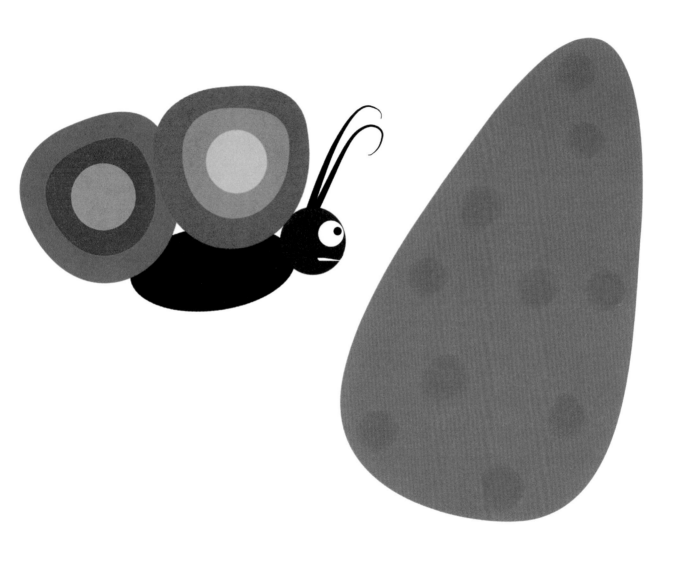

Little bunny, little bunny
Hop! Hop! Hop!

Be mindful of where you're hopping
or you'll hop on to a cow!

Little turtle little turtle
Walk, walk, walk

Be mindful of where you're walking
or you'll walk onto a chicken!

Little bird, little bird
Peep! Peep! Peep!

Mama tells baby bird
it's time to sleep.

Be mindful my precious
little one.

Claudine has been an Occupational Therapist for more than 17 years. She graduated from University of Southern California in 1998 in Occupational Therapy. She currently provides occupational therapy in hospital based settings in the area of trauma/ICU, in-patient psychiatry, and acute rehabilitation. During her career, she has worked in geriatric home health, pediatrics, autism clinics, outpatient clinics and skilled nursing facilities. She has always felt it was very important to gain a wide variety of experiences to work with various disabilities, to understand the different therapy arenas, and to be competent to provide occupational therapy to patients with various neurological, orthopedic and psychiatric disabilities. She feels her two gifts to the world are to provide teaching to those in need and to share her creative talent. Being an occupational therapist has been a perfect career to utilize both of these skills. To move her patients forward, she has found that being mindful of their circumstance helps her to understand their needs to plan their therapeutic goals for progress. Claudine has also found, that educating her patients to be mindful of the task at hand, focusing on their breath, and teaching them to focus, relaxes them as they work together. She has learned, that in any therapy environment, maintaining a mindful connection to her work, being fully engaged with her patient, and staying mindful has been a very successful way to provide therapy. Claudine has earned her certificate in Mindfulness Based Stress Reduction and is a current member of The Academy of Experts in Traumatic Stress in Collaboration with the National Center For Crisis Management. Increasing the ability to remain calm, with increased attention and focus, has tremendous impact to feel peaceful. Her goal is to provide the best occupational therapy to patients and continue to illustrate and publish books that provide a peaceful message . May you have a peaceful journey.

Made in the USA
Middletown, DE
23 August 2018